Practical ways to
CHRISTMAS PLAYS

CC 1841 **012254** 8004

Leabharlanna Atha Cliath
HENRY STREET LIBRARY
Invoice : 02/3070 Price EUR12.45
Title: Practical ways to Chr
Class: 822·008

D0994572

Practical ways to CHRISTMAS PLAYS

Stephanie Jeffs

Text copyright © Stephanie Jeffs 2001
Illustrations copyright © Jane Taylor 2001

The author asserts the moral right
to be identified as the author of this work

Published by
The Bible Reading Fellowship
First Floor, Elsfield Hall
15–17 Elsfield Way, Oxford OX2 8FG
ISBN 1 84101 225 4
First published 2001
10 9 8 7 6 5 4 3 2 1 0
All rights reserved

Acknowledgments
Unless otherwise stated, scripture quotations are taken from the
Good News Bible published by The Bible Societies/HarperCollins
Publishers Ltd, UK © American Bible Society 1966, 1971, 1976,
1992, used with permission

With thanks to the children in Year Six at St Aubyn's School,
Tiverton, Devon for providing the Practical Poems.

A catalogue record for this book is available from the British Library

Printed and bound in Malta

CONTENTS

Introduction

It's that time of year again! The time of year to start thinking and preparing for Christmas, and how best to engage and inspire children to focus their attention (however fleetingly!) on the wonderful truth that God sent Jesus into the world to be its saviour. We hope that these plays will help you to do just that. They are designed to be easy and practical. They are adaptable, suitable for use in schools and churches, with or without a stage and other theatrical paraphernalia, and can be altered to accommodate different-sized cast requirements. Have fun—and think again, in a new way, about Christmas.

Practical Poems

Starry night

On this starry night
Not a stir in sight.
All his clothes threadbare and worn,
Not warm enough
In that cold barn
Only to be dressed in thin yarn.
Born to the Virgin Mary,
A mother so very caring,
As a comfort to men
Both now and then,
Born as the son of Jehovah,
Asleep in the arms of his mother.

JAMES WADDINGTON

Bethlehem

Each year we must return to Bethlehem
To revisit again its Christmas gem.
Will Mary and Joseph let us in
To see the babe and be close to him?

Can we see the silent creatures
And listen to the angel preachers?
Will he wake if the babe we touch?
Will he know that we love him so much?

Rich men may have gifts made with skilful craft,
But love must swell in every heart
For the wondrous child on Christmas morning
As we hear again that miraculous story.

WILLIAM KINGSTON AND TOM TAIT

An echo of two thousand years

Two thousand years and more ago
A loving mother bore her babe,
In a stable, humble and low,
Lit by an oil lamp's quiet glow,
And laid him in a manger of hay
That still had the scent of the summer's day.
Each Christmas time a knock at the door
Is an echo of two thousand years and more.

Now as then a curious crowd
Gathers around, excited and loud.
A reunion of relations
Sweeps through all nations,
And the precious baby stirred
As the echo of two thousand years is heard.

As the sky brightens and dawn fades away
The wandering people depart for the new day.
The baby opens his sleepy eyes once more.
He's so tiny, lying on the crumpled straw.
And the ox and the donkey beside the crib
Are the echo once more of two thousand years.

HARRIET RIX AND LOUISE GILLESPIE

Angels

Our bodies are pure good,
Faces perfectly shaped,
All wonderful symmetry,
Dressed in white silk robes,
All our haloes a glistening gold,
Our bodies surrounded by silver flame.

Our wings can spread
To great lengths,
Soaring the sky,
With a wingspan greater than any bird's.
Yet, we are not individual,
We are made of the purest of pure souls,
Which are merged together,
So that we think as one.

We are but humble messengers for God,
Doing his bidding,
The eternal afterlife, serving God,
In the highest, above the clouds,
Singing his praises.

THOMAS HALL

christmas story

In hot, sandy streets far away,
People look for places to stay.
They've been travelling for many a day:
They've come for the taxes they must pay.

Suddenly on a hillside night,
A star fills the sky, eerily bright,
So that shepherds are blinded by the light,
Which now, filled with angels, turns all to white.

With angels flocking from the sky,
The splendid star shining up high,
Shepherds and kings come hurrying by
To visit the baby in the stable nigh.

Everyone's excited; there is a new king,
He'll rest your spirit from within,
And all your wishes from heaven he'll bring,
So let's all praise him and loudly sing.

HARRIET FRIEND

christmas

A clear night sky
With stars on high,
A cattle trough
Filled with golden straw,
A swinging door.
A special star
Lights a hillside far
Where shepherds sleep
Outside with their sheep.
To this sinful world
On that famous night
Came the Lord of Light,
Jesus.

ALEX CLARE AND JAMES MILNES

How do you spend Christmas?

At Christmas, how do you spend the day?
Are you bound to work as usual?
Are you a farmer, a nurse, a doctor,
Obliged to work, despite the day?
Or can you do nothing and take it easy?

But wherever you are and whatever you do,
You know that God watches over you.
And if you find a moment to pause
You will know the true meaning of Christmas.

MATTHEW HEYWOOD

Advent calendar

As I open my calendar,
I look at the very last door,
And I know that behind it lies
A chocolate bigger than the ones before.

As I peer towards that last door
On this cold Christmas Day,
I see that the very last chocolate
Has, sadly, been taken away.

Then I hear a little gurgle
And see my baby sister there,
Sitting underneath the table,
Chocolate on her face and hair.

And suddenly I remember the true reason why
There's an Advent door for this December morn.
Chocolate and presents are important no more
Compared with the fact that Christ has been born.

ALANNA FRASER AND GRACE GABBITASS

Through the donkey's eyes

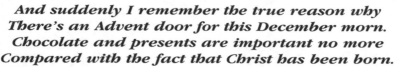

As we drew closer to the inn
I heard the most appalling din.
The innkeeper was sending travellers away,
Even if they tried to pay.

When we asked, the inn was full.
Then he remembered the stable.
Later that night, Mary gave birth,
And God's son was born on earth.

Then came excited visitors:
Shepherds and gift-givers.
These are the words the angels sing:
'Long live Jesus, the newborn king!'

MAX SEYMOUR AND SAM MILDREN

Practical prayers

Lord, when the wise men came from afar
Led to thy cradle by a star,
Then did the shepherds too rejoice,
Instructed by thy angel's voice.
Blest were the wise men in their skill,
And shepherds in their harmless will.
SIDNEY GODOLPHIN (1610–43)

What can I give him,
Poor as I am?
If I were a shepherd,
I would bring a lamb;
If I were a wise man,
I would do my part;
Yet what I can I give him—
Give my heart.
CHRISTINA G. ROSSETTI (1830–94)

Ah, dearest Jesus, holy Child,
Make thee a bed, soft, undefiled,
Within my heart, that it may be
A quiet chamber kept for thee.
MARTIN LUTHER

Father God,
Thank you for sending Jesus
into the world to be our light.
Lord Jesus, please be our light.
Light up our lives, so that we
can be a light to others.
Amen

Loving Father, help us remember
the birth of Jesus, that we may
share in the song of the angels,
the gladness of the shepherds and the
wisdom of the wise men.

Close the door of hate and open the
door of love all over the world.
Let kindness come with every gift and
good desires with every greeting.
Deliver us from evil by the blessing
which Christ brings and teach us to be
merry with clean hearts.

May Christmas morning make us happy
to be your children and Christmas
evening bring us to our beds with
grateful thoughts, forgiving and
forgiven, for Jesus' sake. Amen

Dear Lord Jesus,
We have so much, and so
much to look forward to.
Please help those people who
have very little and nothing to
look forward to.
Please be with them this
Christmas time.
For Jesus' sake. Amen

Lord God,
We thank you for all the excitement of Christmas.
We thank you for parties and fun.
We thank you for cards and parcels.
While we are enjoying ourselves,
help us to remember you.
Amen

Practical costumes

Most of the costumes in this book can be adapted from a simple tunic design. Two rectangles of material, pinned or stitched at the shoulder, make an adequate tunic. Different colours and patterns always make a good effect. Native American tunics should be light brown, with a fringed bottom. Native American patterns and decorations can be drawn on to the fabric. If sleeves are required, make sure that the child wears a suitably coloured T-shirt or long-sleeved top underneath. Then, use a strip of material or a dressing-gown cord as a belt. Make sure that the tunic is not too long, especially if stairs have to be negotiated!

Use a square of fabric folded into a triangle as a headdress, and secure in place with an elasticated Alice band. Old blankets make good cloaks for shepherds, and can be pinned back from the shoulders. Or sling an old sheepskin rug across your back!

Animal ears

For animal ears, make a circle of card about 3cm wide, as a headband to fit each child. Cut ear shapes out of the same colour card and either glue or staple them in place. Use the child's own ears as a guide as to where best to place them.

Lightly padded white baby mittens can make very good sheep's ears. If you are creating animal effects, dress children in suitably coloured jog-pants, leggings or tights, along with a correctly coloured jumper, and suitably coloured gloves or mittens.

Angel wings

Take one large piece of good-quality gold or silver card. Fold it in half and draw the shape of an angel's wing, as in the illustration opposite. Cut out the wing shape, and open up the card. Make two small holes in the middle section of the wings and thread through lengths of gold or silver tinsel. Wrap the tinsel round the angel to keep the wings in shape.

Alternatively, net curtains, gathered in the middle, sewn on to the back of the tunic and attached to the angel's wrists, make very effective 'floaty' wings. Unwanted CDs sewn on to angels' costumes also look very effective. Look out for and save the free ones!

Face painting

Invest in a set of good-quality, water-based face paints. Use a good white base for the sheep, grey for the donkey and so on. Apply the base with a sponge, and use a brush to put in the details. Take care when applying face paints near the eyes, and avoid using red near the eyes altogether. Put a blob of suitable colour on the nose. Add the shape of the mouth, and any whiskers or spots. Generally it is best to put black paint on last. Try out your ideas before the actual performance!

Examples of costumes for basic characters used in the plays are shown on the following pages (13 and 14).

Ideas for the basic characters used in the plays

Doves

Sheep

Cattle

Donkey

Rabbit

Hare

Deer

Ideas for the basic characters used in the plays

Angels

Mary

Joseph

Shepherds

Native American costumes

Practical songs and carols

Most hymn books and song books, like *Songs of Fellowship*, *Mission Praise*, *Junior Praise* and *Carol Praise*, contain a selection of traditional Christmas songs and carols. Listed below are some popular choices, although you may well have some favourites of your own.

Away in a Manger (*CP*)
Come and Join the Celebration (*CP*)
Come On and Celebrate (*S of F*)
Girls and Boys, Leave your Toys (*CP*)
In the Bleak Midwinter (*CP*)

Little Donkey (*CP*)
O Come All Ye Faithful (*CP*)
O Little Town of Bethlehem (*CP*)
See Him Lying on a Bed of Straw (*CP*)
Shine, Jesus, Shine (*S of F*)
Silent Night (*CP*)
Tell Out My Soul (*MP, CP, JP*)
The Angel Gabriel from Heaven Came (*CP*)
The Rocking Carol, or Jesus, Saviour, Holy Child (*CP*)
What Can I Give to the King? (*CP*)
While Shepherds Watched (*CP*)

Practical ways to create effect and tableaux

To create an effective tableau, you need to think who are the most important characters on stage and work outwards. For example, a crib tableau would start with the crib, and maybe Mary. Decide whether you want to have her sitting or standing. Then bring in the next character or group of characters. By the time everyone is in the tableau, they should all be focusing on the main, most important person—not detracting from him or her! Eye contact is vital, so remember to tell the children to use their eyes and look at the most important aspect of the tableau.

Think about all the different levels you can use: lying, sitting, kneeling forward, kneeling up, on one knee, standing, standing alone, standing on tiptoe, standing in a group. Obviously those who are lying or sitting should be at the front of the tableau, and those who are standing at the back. Take an instant photograph, if you can, and see what the scene looks like. Can you see everyone? Does it look like a boring group photo, or an action-packed snapshot of an event?

Once you have decided where everyone is going to be in the tableau, practise moving in and out of the tableau, so that it doesn't become a rugby scrum!

Practical ways to avoid pitfalls

When you rehearse your play, make sure that you view it from the audience's point of view. A general premise must be that if you are on stage you need to be seen and heard. Of course, this means that if you are on stage and not doing what you should be doing, it is likely that you will be seen and heard—only doing the wrong thing!

Avoid having children standing in a straight line on stage. If there are several characters talking together, divide them into smaller groups, and place them in clusters on the stage, so that they 'fill' the space. Make sure that the children do not speak with their backs to the audience and do not stand in front of one another. As a rule, encourage your actors to come 'downstage' as much as possible. Nerves have the effect of pushing everyone to the back, so practise bringing the action forward.

From the outset, make sure that the children take a big, deep breath before they speak, and that they are aware how far their voices need to travel. It is not always possible to rehearse in the same space as the performance, but it is useful to be as familiar with the performance space as possible.

Decide whether or not you are going to have a prompt. In rehearsals, encourage children to help each other out if words are forgotten. In that way they become familiar with the whole play, not just their own part, and learn to improvise dialogue if lines are forgotten. It is worth reminding the cast that most mistakes go unnoticed by an audience, unless someone draws attention to them!

Name: _____

Title of the play: _____

My character: _____

Rehearsal One

* Highlight or underline your words or your part.
* Can you describe your character in three words?
* What do you need to do for next week?
* What do you need to bring for next week?
* What would you like God to do for your group as you take part in this play?

Rehearsal Two

* Highlight or underline your entrances and exits.
* Draw three expressions on the faces below. Which characters need to use these expressions in your play?
* Write down any instructions you might have been given this week.
* Do you need to remember anything for next week?
* What would you like God to do for you as you take part in this play?

Rehearsal Three

* Draw your set in the box below. Make sure you know where your audience is.
* Where do you come on stage? Where do you go off stage? Where do you sit or stand? Mark your positions on the stage using three different colours.
* Draw three expressions which you might have on your face during the play.
* Do you need to remember anything for next week?
* What would you like God to do for the audience as they watch your play?

Rehearsal Four

* Draw your costume in the box below.
  Do you need to find anything?
  Do you need to borrow anything?
* Write a list of any props you need.
* Write down any props you have offered to lend.
* Is there anything you need to find?
* What are the good parts in your play? Write a
  prayer thanking God for the good things you
  have done over the last few weeks.

Rehearsal Five

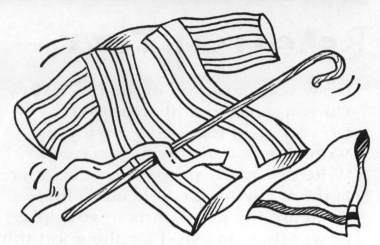

* This is the dress rehearsal. What things do you need to remember before you do the performance?
* Design a ticket or a programme cover in the space below.
* Write a prayer thanking God for Christmas.

Rehearsal Five

On Christmas Night

Age range

Suitable for 7 year olds

INTRODUCTION

If you are looking for a traditional Christmas story, then this nativity play is the one for you. Using strong rhythmic narration and simple acting, this play is suitable for a flexible number of people, especially within the younger age range. It is simply staged, so it can be used in a variety of different venues. The play starts with an empty space and ends up crammed full of all the characters in the Christmas story, plus a few extras. Lines and characters can be deleted as required.

Bible link

Before you begin, read through the Christmas story recorded in Luke 2:1–20 and think about the different characters mentioned in the story. Read through several different versions, and have a look at the different approaches to the Christmas story as re-told in a variety of children's books. Ask God to show you something new in this familiar story and ask that he will show something new to the children too. Follow Mary's example, who 'remembered all these things and thought deeply about them'.

At that time the Emperor Augustus ordered a census to be taken throughout the Roman Empire. When this first census took place, Quirinius was the governor of Syria. Everyone, then, went to register himself, each to his own town.

Joseph went from the town of Nazareth in Galilee to the town of Bethlehem in Judea, the birthplace of King David. Joseph went there because he was a descendant of David. He went to register with Mary, who was promised in marriage to him. She was pregnant, and while they were in Bethlehem, the time came for her to have her baby. She gave birth to her first son, wrapped him in strips of cloth and laid him in a manger—there was no room for them to stay in the inn.

There were some shepherds in that part of the country who were spending the night in the fields, taking care of their flocks. An angel of the Lord appeared to them, and the glory of the Lord shone over them. They were terribly afraid, but the angel said to them, 'Don't be afraid! I am here with good news for you, which will bring great joy to all the people. This very day in David's town your Saviour was born—Christ the Lord! And this is what will prove it to you: you will find a baby wrapped in strips of cloth and lying in a manger.'

Suddenly a great army of heaven's angels appeared with the angel, singing praises to God: 'Glory to God in the highest heaven, and peace on earth to those with whom he is pleased!'

When the angels went away from them back into heaven, the shepherds said to one another, 'Let's go to Bethlehem and see this thing that has happened, which the Lord has told us.'

So they hurried off and found Mary and Joseph, and saw the baby lying in the manger. When the shepherds saw him, they told them what the angel had said about the child. All who heard it were amazed at what the shepherds said. Mary remembered all these things and thought deeply about them. The shepherds went back, singing praises to God for all they had heard and seen; it had been just as the angel had told them.

LUKE 2:1–20

Practical preparation

Read through the play several times before you present it to your group. Try to grasp the rhythm of the text. The key to the success of this play is simplicity. It is an accumulative experience, starting with nothing and ending with everything!

Photocopy the Rehearsal Diary on pages 18–22 and decide how best to use it with your group. Then photocopy enough copies of the play for each child. Alternatively, as there are

Practical staging

All that is needed to perform this play is a space where you can fit all of your characters to create a final Christmas tableau scene. However, the play is eminently suitable for performance in a place where you can use different levels and areas to sustain interest and impact. A church would be wonderful! The stable scene could be created in the chancel. The pulpit could be used by any or all of the moon, stars and angels, as could the lectern. The shepherds could use the aisle as their 'fields'.

Practical costumes

See pages 12–14 for some handy hints about creating costumes. For the animals, you really need to gauge your choice of actors. Younger children will generally not mind dressing up in suitably coloured outfits to represent their animal—for example, brown for the cattle, white for the doves and sheep, grey for the donkey. Masks could be used, but some children do not like to wear them, and prefer to use face paint. Ears, tails and wings are all that is needed to represent the creatures.

Practical start

 Begin by asking the children what they do in their families on Christmas Eve, and then on Christmas night. How do their feelings differ between the two evenings? Are they excited with anticipation on Christmas Eve, and full up with everything good on Christmas night? Ask them to remember those two feelings, as both are part of the Christmas story. Choose a well-illustrated children's picture book of the Christmas story and read it to them. Ask if the children can remember who they have heard about. Think back to the two different emotions.

* When in the story might some of the characters have felt that Christmas Eve feeling?
* When might they have felt that Christmas night feeling?

Then ask the children to imagine who else *might* have been there on that first Christmas night. In pairs or small groups, ask the children to imagine that they are two of those other characters and to devise a quick conversation about what they saw on the first Christmas night. For example, the conversation might be between the moon and the star. A starting line for one might be, 'You'll never guess what I've just seen...'

Practical plot

This really is easy! The story starts in an empty stable and ends up with all the characters worshipping the baby Jesus.

only a few speaking parts, give the narrators a copy of the text, and photocopy the play on to OHP acetates for the actors. This will mean that they will be free to express themselves, rather than having their head in a script that they don't really need.

Look at the carols, songs, poems and prayers (pages 8–11, 15) and decide which you might like to use. This may be a good way of including other children as readers.

Practical casting

This play is very adaptable, and can be subtly changed to suit the needs of your group. It relies on strong, rhythmic narration and simple visual acting.

The Narrators: The narration can be undertaken by one, two, or a chorus of people. The lines have been written in such a way as to indicate a suggested way of dividing the narration. However, although the play is simple, the narration does demand some tight delivery, so good, clear, expressive readers are needed to carry it.

The Cast have minimal lines to learn, but do need to be quick on their cues. The stagehands have nothing to say, so their parts could be 'played' by an adult helper.

Practical props

1 manger
4 stools or blocks to make a simple stable
1 baby doll

On Christmas Night

Cast

Narrator(s)	Stage hands
Cattle	Donkey
Dove(s)	Mary
Joseph	Moon
Star(s)	Sheep
Shepherd(s)	Angel(s)

Narrator: On Christmas night, long, long ago, something very special happened in a stable, far away in a place called Bethlehem.

(Stage hands move blocks or furniture to make a stable)

On Christmas night,
long, long ago…
On Christmas night,
long, long ago…
in a stable in Bethlehem
the cattle were dozing.

(Enter cattle, and settle down in the stable)

Cattle: We're very dozy cattle!
Narrator: On Christmas night,
long, long ago…
in a stable in Bethlehem
the cattle were dozing
and a donkey was snoring.

(Enter donkey)

Donkey:	Snore!
Cattle:	Be quiet! We're trying to doze!
Narrator:	On Christmas night,
	long, long ago…
	in a stable in Bethlehem
	the cattle were dozing
	and a donkey was snoring
	and doves were cooing.

(Enter doves)

Doves:	Coo! Coo!
Donkey:	Snore! Snore!
Cattle:	Doze! Doze!
Narrator:	On Christmas night,
	long, long ago…
	in a stable in Bethlehem
	the cattle were dozing
	and a donkey was snoring
	and doves were cooing
	and a baby was crying!
Doves, cattle and donkey:	A baby was crying?
Narrator:	Yes! A baby was crying!
Doves etc:	Whatever is a baby doing in our stable?

(A 'baby' is placed in the manger)

Narrators:	Listen, and we'll tell you!
	On Christmas night,
	long, long ago…
	in a stable in Bethlehem…
Doves etc:	Yes! We got that bit…
Narrators:	The baby's mother, Mary, was dreaming.

(Enter Mary)

	Her husband, Joseph, was resting.

(Enter Joseph)

	The baby was sleeping.
Doves etc:	The baby was sleeping?
Narrators:	Yes! Jesus was sleeping.
	On Christmas night,
	long, long ago…
	On a Bethlehem hillside
	The moon was shining.

(Enter moon)

Moon:	Shine! Shine!
Narrators:	The stars were twinkling.

(Enter stars)

Stars:	Twinkle! Twinkle!
Narrators:	The sheep were snoozing.

(Enter sheep)

Sheep:	Snooze! Snooze!
Narrators:	The shepherds were watching.

(Enter shepherds)

Doves etc:	The shepherds were watching?
Narrators:	Yes! The shepherds were watching!
Doves etc:	Why were the shepherds watching?
Narrators:	Listen, and we'll tell you!
	On Christmas night, long…
Doves etc:	…long ago. Yes! We've got that bit.
Narrators:	The shepherds were watching their sheep on the hillside, when suddenly they were shaking…
	…quivering…
	…and quaking.
	The night sky was sparkling, and an angel was talking!

(Enter angel)

Doves etc:	An angel was talking?
Narrators:	Yes! An angel was talking!
Doves etc:	What was an angel doing out there on the hillside?
Narrators:	Listen, and we'll tell you!
	On Christmas night…
All:	…long, long ago…

Narrator: An angel was talking to shepherds on the hillside, when suddenly millions of angels…

(Enter angels)

All: Millions of angels?!

Angels: Yes! Millions of angels!

Narrators: …were dancing and singing, praising and singing, God's message bringing.

All: God's message bringing?

Narrators: Yes! God's message bringing!

All: What message bringing?

Narrators: Listen, and we'll tell you! On Christmas night…

All: …long, long ago.

Angel: I've a wonderful message from God in heaven. Some great news for shepherds on the hillside. Some great news for all people everywhere. Some great news to make the sky sparkle. Tonight, in Bethlehem, in a stable…

Cattle: …while cattle were dozing…

Donkey: …and a donkey was snoring…

Doves: …and doves were cooing…

Mary: …and Mary was dreaming…

Joseph: …and Joseph was resting…

Moon: …and the moon was shining…

Stars: …and stars were twinkling…

Sheep: …and sheep were snoozing…

Shepherds: …and shepherds were watching…

Angels: …and angels were singing…

Narrators: Jesus, our saviour, was born.

All: On Christmas night, long, long ago.

(Slowly, all the characters move to form a traditional tableau scene around the crib.)

28

The Two Little Angels

Age range

Suitable for 7–8 year olds

INTRODUCTION

We often think of the Christmas story from the perspective of the characters involved on earth. But this play tells the Christmas story from the perspective of the angels, and two angels in particular. The idea of angels will probably appeal to the younger end of the age range, although there are some 'beefier' parts with angels who are not 'twee' or 'sentimental' but have an understanding of God's plan to save the world.

Before you start work on this play, consider the nature of the angels. To help you do this, read through the poem 'Angels' in the Practical Poems section on page 9.

Bible link

The play is based on the following Bible passages taken from Luke's Gospel.

During the time when Herod was king of Judea, there was a priest named Zechariah, who belonged to the priestly order of Abijah. His wife's name was Elizabeth; she also belonged to a priestly family. They both lived good lives in God's sight and obeyed fully all the Lord's laws and commands. They had no children because Elizabeth could not have any, and she and Zechariah were both very old.

One day Zechariah was doing his work as a priest in the Temple, taking his turn in the daily service. According to the custom followed by the priests, he was chosen by lot to burn incense on the altar. So he went into the Temple of the Lord, while the crowd of people outside prayed during the hour when the incense was burnt.

An angel of the Lord appeared to him, standing on the right of the altar where the incense was burnt. When Zechariah saw him, he was alarmed and felt afraid. But the angel said to him, 'Don't be afraid, Zechariah! God has heard your prayer, and your wife Elizabeth will bear you a son. You are to name him John. How glad and happy you will be, and how happy many others will be when he is born! … He will bring fathers and children together again; he will turn disobedient people back to the way of thinking of the righteous; he will get the Lord's people ready for him.'

Zechariah said to the angel, 'How shall I know if this is so? I am an old man, and my wife is old also.'

'I am Gabriel,' the angel answered. 'I stand in the presence of God, who sent me to speak to you and tell you this good news. But you have not believed my message, which will come true at the right time. Because you have not believed, you will be unable to speak; you will remain silent until the day my promise to you comes true.'
Luke 1:5–14, 17–20

Some time later his wife Elizabeth became pregnant and did not leave the house for five months. 'Now at last the Lord has helped me,' she said. 'He has taken away my public disgrace!'

In the sixth month of Elizabeth's pregnancy God sent the angel Gabriel to a town in Galilee named Nazareth. He had a message for a young woman promised in marriage to a man named Joseph, who was a descendant of King David. Her name was Mary. The angel came to her and said, 'Peace be with you! The Lord is with you and has greatly blessed you!'

Mary was deeply troubled by the angel's message, and she wondered what his words meant. The angel said to her, 'Don't be afraid, Mary; God has been gracious to you. You will become pregnant and give birth to a son, and you will name him Jesus. He will be great and will be called the Son of the Most High God. The Lord God will make him a king, as his ancestor David was, and he will be the king of the descendants of Jacob for ever; his kingdom will never end!'

Mary said to the angel, 'I am a virgin. How, then, can this be?'

The angel answered, 'The Holy Spirit will come on you, and God's power will rest upon you. For this reason the holy child will be called the Son of God. Remember your relative Elizabeth. It is said that she cannot have children, but she herself is now six months pregnant, even though she is very old. For there is nothing that God cannot do.'

'I am the Lord's servant,' said Mary; 'may it happen to me as you have said.' And the angel left her.
LUKE 1:24–38

There were some shepherds in that part of the country who were spending the night in the fields, taking care of their flocks. An angel of the Lord appeared to them, and the glory of the Lord shone over them. They were terribly afraid, but the angel said to them, 'Don't be afraid! I am here with good news for you, which will bring great joy to all the people. This very day in David's town your Saviour was born—Christ the Lord! And this is what will prove it to you: you will find a baby wrapped in strips of cloth and lying in a manger.'

Suddenly a great army of heaven's angels appeared with the angel, singing praises to God: 'Glory to God in the highest heaven, and peace on earth to those with whom he is pleased!'

When the angels went away from them back into heaven, the shepherds said to one another, 'Let's go to Bethlehem and see this thing that has happened, which the Lord has told us.'

So they hurried off and found Mary and Joseph and saw the baby lying in the manger. When the shepherds saw him, they told them what the angel had said about the child. All who heard it were amazed at what the shepherds said. Mary remembered all these things and thought deeply about them. The shepherds went back, singing praises to God for all they had heard and seen; it had been just as the angel had told them.
LUKE 2:8–20

Practical preparation

Read through the play several times. Have a list of your group's names handy as you read the script and think about your choice of casting.

Photocopy the rehearsal diary on pages 18–22, one for each child.

Photocopy the script, punch holes and fasten with tags to form a book.

Look at the carols, songs, poems and prayers (pages 8–11, 15) and decide which you might like to include.

Practical casting

This play is very adaptable, and can accommodate a large cast or a smaller one.

Angelo and Angela: Although these are two young angels, they have the lion's share of the script! They would suit competent, confident performers.

Angels 1–5: If you have fewer people in your group, redistribute the lines. If you need more parts, allocate the lines to a greater number of children. These are small speaking parts.

Gabriel/Michael: Slightly larger speaking parts, which require a certain authority.

Practical props

You will need as many musical instruments as you can find (preferably shiny ones!).

Practical staging

Some stage-blocks or steps would create different levels, but no other scenery is necessary. If you want to create a backdrop, stars, planets and clouds all appear in the text and could be painted on to cloth or flats.

Practical costumes

Refer to the costume ideas on page 12. Each character will need an angel outfit. This needs to be as bright and shiny as possible.

Practical start

Brainstorm with your group the role that the angels play in the Christmas story. Remind them of Zechariah's encounter with Gabriel. On a sheet of paper, ask them to draw their idea of an angel, and then to write down key words that might apply—for example, 'bright', 'scary' and so on. Read through the lists and sift out descriptions that don't apply—for example, 'pretty' and so on—until you have reached an accurate consensus. Here are some key facts:

* Angels are God's messengers
* They know God personally and see him face to face
* They have free will

Once a few key facts have been established, read through the plot of the play.

Practical plot

The play begins with two angels, up in heaven. They wish they could have an adventure—go somewhere other than heaven, and do something important for God. However, they definitely don't want to go to Earth, as they see that it is a place that causes God sadness, and they cannot understand why they should be needed to announce good news to the people of the world.

The Two Little Angels

Cast

Angela	Angel 1
Angelo	Angel 2
Gabriel	Angel 3
Michael	Angel 4
	Angel 5

(Enter Angela and Angelo. They sit down, looking bored)

Angela: Sigh.
Angelo: Humph.
Angela: Oh dear!
Angelo: What shall we do?
Angela: I don't know.
Angelo: I can't think.

Angela: I know! Let's look at the stars!
Angelo: What's the point? They're all beautiful. They're all perfect.
Angela: Not all of them are perfect. They can't be. Some of them shoot.
Angelo: Why don't we plump up a cloud?
Angela: I've already done that. Most of them are self-plumping anyway.
Angelo: Polish a halo?
Angela: (groan)
Angelo: OK, polish two halos?
Angela: But they never really need polishing, do they? Nothing gets dirty or tarnished up here.
Angelo: Well, we could practise.
Angela: Practise what?
Angelo: You know, practise delivering messages. It is what we're supposed to do, after all.

Angela:	But we never get the chance, do we?
Angelo:	You never know, we might do, one day.
Angela:	Well, what would you like to do then?
Angelo:	I don't know. I wish… I wish…
Angela:	Yes…?
Angelo:	I wish, I wish I could do something really exciting, something really important.
Angela:	Like what?
Angelo:	I don't know. I just wish I had something special to do. A job with plenty of opportunities and openings.
Angela:	A sort of heavenly doorman?
Angelo:	No! Not those sort of openings! The sort of openings that lead somewhere, to something exciting…
Angela:	Yeah! I know what you mean. A real adventure. To go somewhere special. The final frontier. To boldly go where no angel has been before, that sort of thing.
Angelo:	Exactly. Just look out there at all that space. All those planets and different universes. There's so much to see. And we haven't seen any of it. Well, only at a distance.

(Enter other angels)

Angel 1:	What are you two up to?
Angelo:	Just looking.
Angel 2:	Looking at what?
Angela:	Out there. It's amazing.
Angelo:	I'd do anything to take just one dive out of heaven into out there.

Angela:	Except there!
Angelo:	Where?
Angela:	You know. There! E.A.R.T.H. The blot on the vista.
Angel 3:	Watch out. Look away if you don't want to see it! It's coming into view any minute now.
All:	Ugh!
Angelo:	It's revolting!
Angela:	It's gross.
Angel 4:	It may be revolting and it may be gross, but God loves it.
Angel 5:	And he made it. In fact…

(There is a sudden commotion off stage as Michael and Gabriel enter)

Angelo:	Oh wow! Here comes Michael.
Angela:	And Gabriel…
Angelo:	I wonder what they are up to.
Michael:	Gather round, everyone. I have a very exciting announcement to make. And you too, little angels. Today is a very important day. God has a very special message that he needs to have delivered.
Angelo/a:	We'll deliver it. We'll deliver it.
Angel 1:	Shh, little angels. Don't interrupt.
Angelo:	But we want to go! We want to leave heaven, just for a bit, and see what else there is.
Angela:	So please… please can we go? We've been practising, haven't we, Angelo?
Angelo:	Yes. Our message delivery record is second to none.
Michael:	I'm sorry, little angels, but Gabriel is going to deliver God's message.
Angelo/a:	Ohh.
Angel 2:	Where's he going?
Angel 3:	Up to the sun?
Angel 4:	Into a black hole?
Angel 1:	Soaring along on a supernova?
Michael:	No! Go on, Gabriel. Tell them where you are going.
Gabriel:	I'm going to Earth.
All (except Gabriel/ Michael):	Earth?!
Angela/o:	Earth?!
Gabriel:	Yes, Earth.
Angel 1:	What do you want to go there for?
Angelo:	It's awful. I've seen it from a distance and it's gross.
Gabriel:	It may look like that from a distance, but if you look at it very, very closely, it's really quite beautiful. At least, that's what God thinks!

(Gabriel rushes off, as if diving down to Earth. The other angels follow him, waving, until all have exited)

(Angelo and Angela enter. They sit down and begin polishing a huge pile of musical instruments, as many as you can muster)

Angelo: Humph.

Angela: What's the matter now?

Angelo: I still don't really get it. I mean, why did Gabriel have to go down to Earth to tell Elizabeth and Mary that they are each going to have a baby? And how are babies going to help people on Earth?

Angela: I don't know. It doesn't make sense. I thought human beings had babies all the time, without us angels having anything to do with it.

Angelo: And why is everyone getting so het up about Earth, when there are so many other beautiful, perfect places out there? Everyone's gone mad.

(Enter Angel 5)

Angel 5: Have you finished polishing yet?

Angela: You must be joking. Have you see how many there are?

Angel 5: Hurry up. We'll be needing them soon and they need to be bright and sparkling.

Angela: He does?

Gabriel: Yes, because he made it and he loves everything he's made.

Angel 2: But it's not how it's made that's the problem. It's what it's crawling with. It's all those things… those… those…

Michael: People?

Angel 3: Yes. People.

Angelo: What's the matter with people?

Angel 4: They're so bad. They're so selfish. Do you know, the only time I've seen God sad is when he's talking about people.

Gabriel: So that's where I am going. I'm going to deliver God's message to some people who live on Earth.

Angel 1: Oh, what does it say? Is God angry? Is he going to tell them off?

Angelo: I don't think I'd like to deliver this message after all.

Gabriel: No. God isn't going to tell them off. He's done that before and they don't take much notice. No, God is going to help them.

Angel 2: How is he going to do that?

Gabriel: He's going to send them a baby.

All: A baby?!

Gabriel: Look, I'll tell you all about it when I get back. Goodbye, everyone.

All: Goodbye, Gabriel.

Angelo:	But they are anyway. I know it's my job to polish, and I'm not trying to get out of it, but what exactly is the point of shining all these instruments when they are already shining?
Angela:	*(Whispering to Angel 5)* I don't know if you've noticed, but everything shines in heaven!
Angel 5:	*(Laughing)* I know! Even we do! But do you know why?
Angelo:	Because we're shiny?
Angel 5:	No! It's because we live in heaven and that's where God is. We shine and sparkle because we're with God all the time and he is with us.
Angela:	I see. But I still don't understand why we have to polish all these…

(Enter all the other angels apart from Michael and Gabriel)

Angel 1:	Where's my harp?
Angel 2:	Is my flute ready?
Angel 3:	Please may I have my trumpet?
Angel 4:	Is that my triangle?
Angela:	Yes, yes, yes. But what's the hurry?
Angel 1:	We need them.
Angel 2:	We've been asked to play some wonderful music.
Angel 3:	And to help deliver an amazing message.

Angela/o:	Can we come? Can we come?
Angelo:	We've always wanted to go somewhere, and to have an adventure.
Angela:	We've always wanted to deliver a message.
Angel 5:	Of course you must come. We're all going. Come on.
Angelo:	But where are we going?
Angel 5:	Earth.
Angela:	Earth! Ergh! I don't want to go there! It's revolting! It's horrid!
Angelo:	That's far too scary. I think I'll stay here, at home.
Angela:	Do you mean to say we've been polishing these instruments so that you can take them down to Earth?
Angelo:	They'll be filthy in micro-seconds.

(Gabriel and Michael enter.)

Michael:	Are you ready, everyone?
All:	Yes.
Gabriel:	Has everyone got their instruments?
All:	Yes.

(Everyone holds up an instrument except Angelo and Angela)

Gabriel:	Good. But what about you two? What are you going to play?
Angelo:	Nothing.
Angela:	We're not going!
All:	Not going?
Michael:	Oh but you must go, little angels. You've always wanted to travel.
Gabriel:	And you've always wanted to deliver a message. This is your chance. There'll never be another like it. Ever.
Angelo:	But why do we have to go to Earth, of all places? I wouldn't mind going somewhere else. Mars? Pluto? Even Jupiter. But not Earth.
Michael:	But Earth is very special. God made the planet Earth and he loves it. He made the people who live there and he loves them too.
Angela:	But they make him so sad. Why does he keep on loving them?
Gabriel:	Because that's what God's like, isn't it? He keeps on loving. He keeps on shining.
Michael:	And now God is going to go there himself.
Angelo:	What? He's leaving heaven to live on Earth?

Michael: So, are you coming, little angels, or are you staying here?

Angela: Wow! Fancy God *choosing* to go down to Earth!

Angelo: And *staying* there!

Angela: If God is prepared to go to Earth, don't you think we should be too?

Angelo: I'm glad I polished those instruments. I hope they sparkle and shine. I hope they tell everyone that God has come to Earth.

(Exit all)

Gabriel: God is going to Earth to live as a human being, so that he knows what it's like and how he can help them. He's going to be born tonight as a little baby, and he needs us to tell the people what he has done.

Gabriel: *(Off stage)* Don't be afraid! I am here with good news for you, which will bring great joy to all people. This very day in David's town your Saviour was born— Christ the Lord!

Angels: *(In unison off stage)* Glory to God in the highest heaven, and peace on earth to those with whom he is pleased!

The Christmas Rebel

Age range

Suitable for 8–9 year olds

INTRODUCTION

The phrase 'I don't want to' is one that is heard in most homes! And it's a phrase that recurs in this nativity play within a play. Here is Christmas seen through the eyes of a rebel. Charlie (male or female) is just plain awkward. While everyone else is happy to play their part in the play, Charlie digs in his/her heels and refuses to comply. In the end s/he is left with the part of the donkey, and comes to realize that his/her part is not so bad after all. Perhaps it is worth considering who the rebels are in your group! Talk about things we are all inclined to rebel against, and lead into discussing what God's plans might be for each of us.

Bible link

As you prepare for Christmas, take time to reflect how Jesus was God's plan to save us from the consequences of our rebellion. The following Bible passage may help.

The people who walked in darkness have seen a great light. They lived in a land of shadows, but now light is shining on them. You have given them great joy, Lord; you have made them happy… [For] a child is born to us! A son is given to us! And he will be our ruler. He will be called, 'Wonderful Counsellor', 'Mighty God', Eternal Father', 'Prince of Peace'. His royal power will continue to grow; his kingdom will always be at peace. He will rule as King David's successor, basing his power on right and justice, from now until the end of time. The Lord Almighty is determined to do all this.
ISAIAH 9:2–3, 6–7

Practical preparation

After you have read the play through yourself several times, photocopy the script so that each child can have a copy. Using a hole punch and bootlace tags, put it together to form a book, so that it is easy for the children to turn the pages.

Photocopy the rehearsal diary on pages 18–22. If you have already decided upon the number of sessions you will use to rehearse the play, decide in advance whether to photocopy the whole rehearsal diary and attach it to the script from the outset, or to copy the appropriate page for use at each separate rehearsal.

Look at the songs and carols suggested in the script, and make sure you have the music and a suitable accompanist. You may need to distribute the words of the songs or carols so that they are familiar, and decide when you can rehearse them. Alternatively, you may wish to insert songs of your own choosing instead.

Practical casting

This play requires some strong acting and competent line learning. It does not rely on narration, and will demand input from the performers outside of rehearsal time.

However, the 'adult' role could be performed by an adult leader if it was felt that the text was too demanding for individual children within your group.

Miss/Mr Polly: This role could be played by an adult helper. Whoever plays the part should have the appropriate gravitas.

Charlie: The awkward member of the cast, who wants everything their own way. This would suit a confident child.

The Cast: The rest of the cast are all children who act out various parts in the nativity story. Everyone has a speaking part, including the company of angels, who could speak their lines in unison. All the characters (apart from Mary, Joseph and the shepherds) can be played by characters of either sex. Alter the names as appropriate.

Practical props

As this play is about a group of children rehearsing a play, the costumes and props need only to be tokens.

1 scroll
1 halo
1 angel's wings
Shepherds' crooks
1 fire
1 sheep
A few stools or a small bench
1 manger

Practical staging

Because of the nature of this play, the whole cast could be on stage all the time, sitting in a semi-circle at the back of the stage, and coming forward to take part in the action at the right time. Although this is very simple and effective, it may demand too much concentration from your group, in which case you might want to sit them on the floor to the side of your stage area and direct them on to the stage at the appropriate place in the script.

Practical costumes

Look at pages 12–14 for some ideas about costuming. Remember that this play demands simplicity, so costumes need to be easy and simple to put on, as the actors change from being children in the cast to children performing a play, very quickly. It might then, as with the props, be better to suggest the complete costume by choosing a token outfit for your actors. For example:

Mary: blue headdress
Joseph, shepherds: simple cloaks
Innkeeper: apron

Practical start

You will need to know your group's ability before starting this play. Bring a selection of token costumes and props to the first session. Familiarize your group with them by playing one of the following games.

* Kim's game: Put the props and token costumes on the floor or a table where everyone can see them. Give the group one minute to memorize the items. Next, cover the items with a cloth, or remove them from view. The children now have a further minute to write down the items. With younger children, give each child a turn to tell the group one item they have remembered.

* Sit in a circle and pass round a piece of material, which will eventually become a cloak. As each person takes hold of it, ask them to do something different with it— for example, wear it in a different way, clean something with it, use it as a pillow, a cover, a bag, and so on. Explain how valuable a cloak was to its owner in biblical times and all the different uses it had.

* Sit in a circle. Put the costumes and props in the middle. Explain which characters they belong to in the Christmas story. Take it in turns to throw the dice. Anyone who throws a six has to put on a costume and mime being that character until another six is thrown and another participant takes over.

Introduce the play by telling the children the title. What sort of a person do they think the Christmas rebel might be?

Practical plot

When Miss Polly wants to put on a Christmas play, all the cast are very enthusiastic—except one! Charlie just doesn't want to do anything s/he is asked to. S/he is really very awkward. But when the only part left is that of the donkey, Charlie becomes aware of the importance of what happened in the stable on that first Christmas night.

The Christmas Rebel

Cast

Charlie	Mary
Miss/Mr Polly	Joseph
Children comprising:	Shepherd 1
Rajiv	Shepherd 2
Edward	Shepherd 3
Graham	Angel 1
Martha	Angels
Jason	(flexible number)
George	

(The whole class are assembled round the stage, as if in the final stages of a play rehearsal)

Miss Polly: Well, everybody. This is it! Our last chance to get this right. Just remember what happened on that first Christmas night, and what a very special story it is! Do your best. Everyone has an important job to do. Get to your positions.

(Everyone moves)

Are you ready, Charlie? Take a nice big breath. 1, 2, 3… begin.

(Charlie just stands there)

Come along, Charlie. Take a nice big breath and off you go!

Charlie: *(Muttering)* Don't want to! Being a narrator isn't very important!

Miss Polly: I couldn't hear that, Charlie, and if I can't hear it, nobody at the back will be able to hear it either. One more time…

(Charlie looks sulky)

Oh Charlie! Don't be awkward. You come and take Charlie's part, Rajiv. We'll have to find something else for Charlie to do.

(Miss Polly leads Charlie off stage and Rajiv and Edward move into the narrators' positions downstage)

42

Rajiv:	Have you ever wondered what happened on that first Christmas night? This is our story of what happened in a remote part of the Roman Empire, over two thousand years ago.
Edward:	There was once a young woman called Mary. She lived in the small Galilean village of Nazareth, where she was engaged to be married to a carpenter called Joseph.

(Enter Mary. She begins to sweep the room. Charlie enters with Miss Polly. S/he is dressed in an angel's costume and is looking very cross)

Miss Polly:	Come on, Charlie. Off you go. Go and tell Mary your message.
Charlie:	I don't want to!
Miss Polly:	And try and look happy. Angels don't have cross faces.
Charlie:	This one does! I don't want to be an angel. I don't want to give a message. I want to do something important.
Miss Polly, Rajiv, Edward and Mary:	Oh Charlie! Don't be awkward!
Miss Polly:	The angel is important. Very important. But never mind, Charlie. If you don't want to, I'm sure somebody else would like to have a go. Would you mind, Graham?

(Graham takes any suitable angel 'props' off Charlie and moves downstage)

Graham:	Hello, Mary!
Mary:	Who are you? Whatever do you want?
Graham:	I am the angel Gabriel, God's messenger. I have some wonderful news for you. You are going to have a very special baby. He will be God's own son, his saviour for the whole world. You will give him the name Jesus.
Mary:	I don't understand. How can this happen?
Graham:	The Holy Spirit will come on you, and God's power will rest upon you. God really will be the baby's father and Jesus will be his son.
Mary:	I still don't fully understand. But I do believe what you have told me. I am bursting with the news that God has given me. God has kept his promise to send the world his saviour.

CAROL/SONG: The Angel Gabriel from Heaven Came
Tell Out, My Soul (verse 1)

(All the children gather round Miss Polly)

Miss Polly:	Well done, everyone. Wasn't that good? Now who can tell me what happens next?

(Everyone except Charlie puts their hands up)

	Can you tell us, Charlie?
Charlie:	Don't want to!
Miss Polly:	Oh Charlie! Don't be awkward!
Miss Polly:	Come on, Martha, you tell us.
Martha:	*(She stands up and speaks her lines with great excitement as if recounting the story to her friends, rather than narrating a play)* Well, some time after the angel had spoken to Mary, the Roman Emperor, Caesar Augustus, wanted to know how many people lived in his empire and so he decided to count them all. He ordered that everyone should go to their family town to register their names.

Jason: *(Springing spontaneously to his feet, taking on the role of Emperor)* I, Caesar Augustus, decree that everyone must go to register their names.

(While Martha recounts the next part of the story, the children playing the parts of Mary and Joseph move as though making their journey)

Martha: So Mary and her husband Joseph left the village of Nazareth and made the long journey to Bethlehem. Poor Mary knew that she was going to have her baby very soon, and she was very tired. Joseph was so relieved to see the lights of Bethlehem in the distance.

CAROL: Little donkey

Miss Polly: Lovely, Martha. Come along, Mary and Joseph, you know what happens next.
Mary/Joseph: Yes, Miss Polly.
Miss Polly: Good. So all we need now is the innkeeper. How about it, Charlie?
Charlie: I don't want to! The innkeeper only has a little bit to do! I don't want to have to work hard, serving people, waiting on them hand and foot!
All: Oh, Charlie! Don't be awkward!
George: I know working in the inn must have been hard work, but it must have been exciting as well, meeting all those people from different places. And seeing Mary and Joseph.
Miss Polly: I think you're right, George. So it looks as though it's up to you!

(George takes up the role of the innkeeper)

George: Oh, it's so busy! There's so much to do. I've never seen so many people in Bethlehem.
Joseph: Excuse me, is this the inn?
George: It is. But I hope you don't expect to find a room here. We are completely full up. I'm so sorry. There isn't a space anywhere.
Joseph: Oh dear! I don't know what to do. My wife is going to have a baby very soon, and I must find a place where she can rest.

George: Yes, of course you must. I really don't know what to suggest… unless… I know! We have a stable you could use. It's not ideal but…
Joseph: Thank you! I'm most grateful. Thank you.

CAROL: O Little Town of Bethlehem

Miss Polly: So, as Mary and Joseph were settling into the stable, there was a group of shepherds on the hillside. Off you go, shepherds.

(Shepherds get into positions, bringing with them their props, for example, fire, crooks and toy sheep)

Shep 1: It's cold tonight.
Shep 2: Give the fire a prod, Seth.
Shep 3: Go on, Seth, give the fire a prod.
Shep 1: He can't!
Miss Polly: Why can't he?
Shep 2: He's not here.
Miss Polly: Who's the shepherd? Oh Charlie! You're supposed to be the shepherd.
Charlie: Don't want to be a shepherd. I don't want to sit out on a cold, wet hillside watching stupid sheep. It's boring!
All: Oh Charlie! Don't be awkward!
Shep 1: We don't stay out all night! We run down to Bethlehem, remember?

Shep 2: And we forget about being outside in the cold and the damp, because we see the angels!

Shep 3: And we stop being bored because we hear the most exciting news!

(Angel moves forward)

Angel 1: Listen! I have the most wonderful news, which is not just for you, but for the whole world. Tonight, while you have been out here on the hillside, a baby has been born in Bethlehem. He is God's own son, his saviour for the whole world. You can go and see him for yourselves. You will find him wrapped up in strips of cloth, lying in a manger!

(The other angels move into the action)

Angels: Glory!
Glory!
Glory to God in heaven!
Peace!
Peace!
Peace has come to earth!

Shep 1: Wow! Did you hear what the angels said?

Shep 2: What are we waiting for? Come on!

Shep 3: What a shame that Seth has missed it! Let's see this baby for ourselves.

Miss Polly: So the shepherds left the hillside and their sheep, and ran as quickly as they could to Bethlehem. They searched everywhere until they found the stable. Get the stable ready, everyone.

(Cast moves crib into position)

Hmm… there's something missing.

George: Don't we need some animals in the stable?

Rajiv: Yes, an ox or an ass.

Edward: Or maybe a donkey…?

Miss Polly: You're right! The stable was the animals' home. It was a very strange place for such an amazing baby to be born! But, everyone's done something. Who could be the donkey…?

All: Charlie!

Miss Polly: Oh, yes! Charlie! You can be the donkey!

Charlie: I don't want to be the donkey! I don't want to be in a smelly, stinky stable. The donkey's not important…

All: Oh Charlie! Don't be awkward!

Charlie: I'm not awkward! I just don't want to be the donkey, that's all.

Edward: You are awkward!

Charlie: I'm not!

Rajiv: Well, you didn't want to tell the story.

Martha: You didn't want to tell everyone what happened on that first Christmas time.

Graham: And you didn't want to be the angel. You didn't think it was important enough.

Mary: You didn't want to tell Mary the amazing news that she was going to have such a special baby.

George: And you didn't want to be the innkeeper. It was too hard work, you said.

Shep 1: And you didn't want to be a shepherd.

Shep 2: You didn't want to hear the angel's wonderful news.

Shep 3: You said it would be boring. And you missed everything.

Angels: And you didn't want to listen to us praising God.

45

Joseph: So now you've got to be the donkey. We need a donkey in the stable.

Miss Polly: Oh Charlie! If only you hadn't been awkward, you could have done such exciting things! All those amazing things that happened, and you missed it!

Charlie: All right! All right! I'll do it! I'll be the donkey!

All: Oh Charlie!

(Charlie grabs the donkey costume from Miss Polly and sulkily takes up his/her position in the stable)

Miss Polly: So where we? Ah yes. The stable.

(Mary and Joseph take up their positions beside the manger)

Mary: Welcome to the world, Jesus.

Joseph: Welcome to our world, Jesus, God's own son.

(Shepherds enter and gather around the manger)

Shep 1: The angel said that we would find him here.

Shep 2: They said God's son was good news for the whole world.

Shep 3: And so we've come to worship him. We've come to worship Jesus, who was born in a stable!

(Enter angels)

Angels: Glory to God in heaven. God's saviour has been born.

Charlie: *(Springing up out of his/her place)* Yippee!

All: Oh Charlie!

Charlie: Whoopee!

All: Oh Charlie! Don't be awkward!

Charlie: I'm not being awkward! This time I'm really not. I'm very, very happy!

All: You are? Oh Charlie!

Charlie: I'm *glad* I am the donkey! I'm glad I'm in the stable.

Mary: Oh Charlie! What's made you change your mind?

Charlie: You said that I'd missed doing all those amazing things, but now I see that the most amazing thing happened in the stable. It didn't happen in Nazareth and it didn't happen at the inn. It didn't happen on the hillside, either. The most amazing thing in the whole world happened that night in the stable. And that's where I was. Jesus, God's son, was born in a stinky, smelly stable, and I'm glad that I was there to see it!

All: **We're glad too, Charlie!**

CAROL: Away in a Manger

The Startled Shepherd

Age range

Suitable for 7–11 year olds

INTRODUCTION

Have you ever wondered what that first Christmas night was like from the shepherds' point of view? Plenty of people have thought about it over the years. Well, here is a play which focuses on the shepherds, and one shepherd in particular, Benjamin. However, apart from having light-hearted, comic elements, which will appeal to the 7–11 age group, its theme is the surprising and staggering way in which God chose to come into our world. It is the most amazing thought that God chose to leave all the wonders of heaven to come to earth as a little baby.

Bible links

Before you start work on the play, and before you introduce it to your group, take time to reflect on the incredible nature of God's incarnation, using these verses from Philippians:

He always had the nature of God, but did not think that by force he should try to remain equal with God. Instead of this, of his own free will he gave up all he had, and took the nature of a servant. He became like a human being and appeared in human likeness. He was humble and walked the path of obedience all the way to death—his death on the cross.

PHILIPPIANS 2:6–8

The story of the play is based on the following passage:

There were some shepherds in that part of the country who were spending the night in the fields, taking care of their flocks. An angel of the Lord appeared to them, and the glory of the Lord shone over them. They were terribly afraid, but the angel said to them, 'Don't be afraid! I am here with good news for you, which will bring great joy to all the people. This very day in David's town your Saviour was born—Christ the Lord! And this is what will prove it to you: you will find a baby wrapped in strips of cloth and lying in a manger.'

Suddenly a great army of heaven's angels appeared with the angel, singing praises to God: 'Glory to God in the highest heaven, and peace on earth to those with whom he is pleased!'

When the angels went away from them back into heaven, the shepherds said to one another, 'Let's go to Bethlehem and see this thing that has happened, which the Lord has told us.'

So they hurried off and found Mary and Joseph and saw the baby lying in the manger. When the shepherds saw him, they told them what the angel had said about the child. All who heard it were amazed at what the shepherds said. Mary remembered all these things and thought deeply about them. The shepherds went back, singing praises to God for all they had heard and seen; it had been just as the angel had told them.

LUKE 2:8–20

Practical preparation

Before you begin, make sure that you have read through the play two or three times, with your group in mind.

Photocopy the rehearsal diary on pages 18–22, so that each child can have a copy to attach to his or her script. This will be a handy reminder of the rehearsals as well as a reminder of some of the pertinent issues in the story.

Photocopy enough copies of the play for each child. Collate the pages by using a hole punch and bootlace tags to make a book, rather than stapling at the corner, which can be difficult when turning over the page and acting at the same time.

Look at the list of songs and carols on page 15 and at the selection of poems and prayers (pages 18–22). Decide which, if any, you want to include in your production.

Practical casting

Adapt the play to suit the needs of your group. The script has fast-moving dialogue and there is quite a bit of stage movement which will need to be rehearsed if it is to be effective. There are some suggested movements in the stage directions in the script.

The Narrators: The narration can be undertaken by one, two, or several voices, either speaking in unison (always effective if amplification is a problem) or by saying a line each, as laid out in the script.

Luke, Reuben, Seth, Jacob: Lively acting is required, as well as the ability to learn some lines and react to cues. Lines can be divided between a larger group of shepherds if necessary.

Benjamin This character stands alone: at the beginning he is confident and assured, but at the end is stunned into wondrous silence. He should be played by someone with a good sense of fun, who doesn't mind standing out.

Sheep: The sheep could be a welcome humorous addition, if your group is up to it, and if you need to accommodate a large cast. Alternatively they can be replaced by the toy variety, with their line(s) cut.

Bear: Just a small growling part for someone with a sense of fun. Could easily be doubled up with another character.

Robbers: An indeterminate number of robbers, with lines that can be divided between your cast or spoken in unison.

Angel(s): One angel has the bulk of the lines and should be someone with a strong, clear voice. The other angels follow his or her lead.

Mary/Joseph: Non-speaking but nevertheless essential parts!

Practical props

1 crook
1 pair of open sandals
1 toy sheep (if required)
1 doll wrapped in sheeting
1 manger (optional)
2 stools

Practical staging

All you need for most drama is an empty space. However, it would be good to consider having somewhere where the robbers can hide— either some upturned blocks to represent rocks and bushes, or some simple lightweight scenery. Just cut out some sheets of polystyrene in the shapes you require (see drawing) and paint them the appropriate colour. Either prop up against blocks, or glue two polystyrene wedges to the reverse to make a stand.

Practical costumes

Each of the shepherds needs a suitable outfit consisting of a tunic, headdress, belt and cloak (see pages 12–14). Seth needs a pair of sandals. Alternatively, the shepherds could be dressed in modern-day attire —jeans, barbours and wellies. If using wellies, change Seth's words in the script.

Use face paints for the character playing the bear, and make a pair of ears, attached to a headband. S/he should wear brown, woolly clothes, and brown slipper-socks and gloves. The sheep are dressed in the same type of costume, except in white, with white ears and white face paint, socks and gloves. A fur waistcoat would add to the effect. The angels can wear white clothes, decorated with tinsel, or a white tunic along similar lines to the shepherd's costume. The robbers could be dressed as modern-day stereotypical robbers with striped clothes, eye masks and swag bags. Alternatively they could have simple tunics and headbands.

Practical start

 Before casting the parts, whet your group's appetite and get them thinking about the Christmas story from the shepherds' point of view.

You never know, they may well come up with some pertinent additions to the text! Read the Bible account of the story from Luke 2:8–20 in a couple of different versions. Divide into groups and ask the children to imagine that they were shepherds out on the hillside that first Christmas night. How would they have felt? What would they have been doing? What sort of things would they have been chatting about? If you have time, encourage the children to improvise their own scenes and show them to the group. Brainstorm any points arising from the improvisations which might be handy to know. Some useful pointers are:

* The shepherds were thought of as the lowest of the low in society because they worked with animals all the time and couldn't observe the Jewish cleansing rituals properly.
* The work was hard. Shepherds were totally responsible for their master's sheep 24 hours a day.
* They were the first people to hear the news of Jesus' birth and they were simple, uneducated men.

Read the narrator's first speech and, in groups, ask the children to hypothesize what happens next. Then explain the plot of the play.

Practical plot

This is a play about a group of shepherds who happen to be on the hills outside Bethlehem on the night when Jesus is born. The story starts with the chief shepherd, Benjamin. Benjamin is different from all the other shepherds because he is never, ever taken by surprise. It doesn't matter whether he is faced with a wild animal or a gang of robbers, Benjamin is always ready and waiting. However, one night he sees some angels and hears the message that they bring. For the first time in his life, Benjamin is surprised as the enormity of Jesus' birth sinks in.

The Startled Shepherd

Cast

Narrator(s)	Benjamin
Luke	Reuben
Seth	Jacob
Sheep	Bear
Robber(s)	Angel(s)

(The narrator(s) stand at one side of the stage, in a group facing the audience)

Narrator: Once upon a time, a long, long time ago, there was a shepherd called Benjamin.

(Benjamin moves forward)

He was very, very big…

(Stands on tiptoe)

…and he was very, very strong…

(Flexes his muscles)

…and nothing ever frightened him or made him afraid.

(Takes an aggressive stance)

Benjamin: Nothing ever surprises me!

51

(Enter shepherds)

Shepherds: Nothing ever startles Benjamin.

(Enter sheep on to stage. They settle themselves)

Narrator: One day, Benjamin and his friends were looking after their sheep. They didn't notice anything strange.

(Bear creeps on to stage)

Luke: Help, there's a bear!
Reuben: Where?
Seth: Over there!
Jacob: Look out, Benjamin!

(Bear creeps up behind Benjamin)

Benjamin: Don't worry, I'm not afraid!
Shepherds: He's behind you!

(Bear taps Benjamin on the shoulder)

Bear: Grr!
Benjamin: Grraaah!
Bear: Aaargh!

(Bear runs off, terrified)

Benjamin: Ahaha! That gave you a fright. You see, I'm not afraid. Nothing ever startles or surprises me.

Luke: My teeth are chattering.
Benjamin: My teeth never chatter!
Shepherds: Nothing ever startles Benjamin.
Narrator: One afternoon, Benjamin and his friends had moved to find new pasture, so that they could feed their sheep.

(Shepherds standing in a line, walking on the spot in unison)

They walked up the hillside…

(Walking on tiptoe)

…up and down the hillside…

(Walking on tiptoe and then with knees bent)

…down and up…
…up and down…
Shepherds: Are we nearly there yet?
Sheep: Are we nearly there yet?
Benjamin: We're very nearly there.
Narrator: …until they reached the hills just outside the little town of Bethlehem. At last they settled down, to rest their tired feet.

(Everyone sits down, including the sheep, to rub their feet. Seth takes off his sandals. Suddenly everyone, including the sheep, sniff the air)

Luke: Errgh! There's something very odd here.
Reuben: A very funny odour.
Jacob: Like a rotten Galilean fish.
Seth: And it's getting closer!
Luke: It's getting up my nose!
Reuben: I can hardly breathe!
Shepherds: Whatever can it be?!
Benjamin: Keep calm, everyone. Don't worry! I will sort it! Remember, I am Benjamin. I am not afraid.
Shepherds: Be careful, Benjamin!

(They huddle together, while Benjamin hooks the sandal with his crook)

Benjamin: Ahaha! It was only Seth's smelly sandal. You see, I'm not afraid! Nothing ever startles or surprises me!
Reuben: My knees are knocking.
Benjamin: My knees never knock!
Shepherds: Nothing ever startles Benjamin.
Narrator: The shepherds settled down.

52

(The actors follow the instructions from the narrator)

	They put the sheep in the pen, and Seth's sandal in the bushes!
Seth:	Hey!
Narrator:	And they settled down for the evening.
Shepherds:	Let's settle down for the evening.
Narrator:	They played hunt the ewe...

(Shepherds look for ewe and find it in an unlikely place, perhaps 'planted' somewhere in the audience)

...and counted the sheep.

(Shepherds count members of the audience)

	It was hard work out on the hillside. After all, anything could happen.
Luke:	*(Coughing)* Help me! Help me!
Shepherds:	Whatever is the matter?
Luke:	I think I must have swallowed something. I'm choking. I feel as if I'd swallowed a sheep!
Shepherds:	Hang on a minute, Luke. Whatever shall we do?

(Shepherds run around in panic and disarray, while Benjamin remains calm)

Benjamin:	Don't panic, Luke. *(Slapping Luke on the back)* That should make you better.
Luke:	Thank you, thank you, Benjamin. You always know what to do.
Benjamin:	Yes, I always seem to. Nothing ever startles me. Now tell me, how do *ewe* feel?
Luke:	Not too baaad!
Shepherds:	Groan!
Narrator:	After such excitement, the shepherds decided to settle down for the evening again. Suddenly they heard a noise.
Luke:	Shh! I think I heard a noise.
Narrator:	They heard a rustling in the bushes.
Reuben:	Shh! I think I heard a rustling in the bushes.
Narrator:	They heard footsteps creeping up the hillside.
Jacob:	Shh! I think I can hear footsteps creeping up the hillside!
Narrator:	In the darkness of the evening, creeping up the hillside... up and down the hillside... a gang of fearsome robbers... were out to steal some sheep.
Shepherds:	Oh no! A gang of fearsome robbers are out to steal our sheep!

(The shepherds huddle together)

| **Benjamin:** | I think a gang of fearsome robbers are about to steal our sheep. |

Robbers: *(Springing out between the shepherds and their sheep)* We're a gang of fearsome robbers and we're out to steal your sheep. Watch out! This is a ram raid! Hand over your sheep!

(Benjamin creeps off in the direction where the sandal was thrown, which must be behind the robbers)

Luke: Oh no! Whatever shall we do?

Seth: *(Whispering)* Don't panic, everybody! Benjamin will sort it.

Jacob: Keep calm and wait for Benjamin.

Reuben: Wherever he may be.

(Benjamin enters behind robbers, holding Seth's sandal as if it were a weapon)

Benjamin: Ahaha! All right, you fearsome robbers! Your ram raid's over. The game is up for ewe. Now disappear quickly before I lock you in the pen.

Robber: Cor! What's happening? What's that awful smell?

Benjamin: Now go, before I get you.

Robbers: Come on, let's make a dash for it.
(As they run off) I didn't fancy lamb for tea anyway.
How about fish?
You must be joking, after that smell…

Shepherds: Well done, Benjamin! *(Gathering round him)*

Luke: However do you do it?

Jacob: Aren't you ever frightened?

Reuben: Aren't you ever afraid?

Benjamin: It was only a gang of fearsome robbers, and my name's Benjamin and I'm never afraid. Nothing ever frightens me or takes me by surprise.

Jacob: My body's shaking.

Benjamin: My body never shakes!

Shepherds: Nothing ever startles Benjamin.

Narrators: The shepherds settled down for the evening once again.
The sky was very dark.
And stars twinkled in the sky.
This time they didn't play.
This time they didn't chat.
This time they didn't even choke.
They lay down in front of the pen, and began to go to sleep.
Suddenly a bright light appeared in the sky.

Luke: Look, there's a bright light in the sky.

Reuben: So there is. It's getting bigger.

Seth: It's coming down towards us.

Luke: It's really getting closer.

Reuben: Whatever can it be?

Seth: Wake up, Benjamin!

(The shepherds shake Benjamin)

Benjamin: *(Getting up)* Now, tell me what's the matter. What do you want sorting? *(Looking surprised)* Why, goodness gracious me!

(Benjamin listens to the whole of this section with his mouth wide open, while the other shepherds remain 'together')

(Enter angel, with a cymbal clash if possible)

Angel: Hello, you shepherds, out there on the hillside. I've come to tell you the most exciting news! Do not be afraid!
Luke: Wow! Did you see that!
Seth: It must be an angel!
Reuben: He's come to us from heaven.
Benjamin: Daa… err… ugh.
Angel: There's no need to be afraid. Tonight, in Bethlehem, a baby boy has been born. He is a very special baby. He is God's own son—his saviour for the whole world.
Luke: Wow! Did you hear that?
Seth: A baby has been born.
Reuben: God's saviour for the world.
Benjamin: Daa… err… ugh.
Angel: Go and see him for yourselves. He's fast asleep in a manger.

(Enter host of angels)

Luke: Wow! The sky is full of angels!
Seth: They're singing and they're dancing!
Reuben: I've never seen anything like it.

Angels: God has sent his saviour down to earth today!

(Exit angels. Reuben, Luke and Seth are very excited, hopping around, clapping their hands and so on. Benjamin is motionless in the middle, with his mouth still open)

Seth: Come on!
Reuben: Let's go!
Luke: Let's see this baby for ourselves.
Shepherds: Come on, Benjamin! *(Turning to look at him)*
Reuben: Are you all right, Benjamin? Your eyes look odd.
Seth: So does your mouth.
Luke: In fact, you look rather shocked.
Seth: Surprised.
Reuben: Startled, even.
Shepherds: But nothing ever startles Benjamin!
Benjamin: This did! That God should send angels to us on the hillside is amazing. That he should send a saviour is surprising. But that God's Son should be born as a little baby is quite, quite stunning!

(Enter Mary and Joseph. They sit on the stools and Mary nurses her 'baby'. The shepherds slowly turn round to look at the baby and kneel in traditional tableau style)

Benjamin: Jesus is God's wonderful surprise for the whole world.
Shepherds: He even startled Benjamin!

Grandfather's Wigwam

Age range

Suitable for 7–11 year olds

INTRODUCTION

Have you ever considered what might happen if you took the main events in the Christmas story and put them in a different setting and a different culture? This play, based on a traditional Native American tale, aims to do just that, and in so doing highlights the universal nature of the Christmas story. God sent Jesus into the world for all the people of the world, whatever the place, whatever the culture.

Bible link

At this point, reflect upon Jesus' words to Nicodemus. This passage shows that the Christmas story is for everyone, everywhere, whoever they are or wherever they live.

For God loved the world so much that he gave his only Son, so that everyone who believes in him may have eternal life.
JOHN 3:16

Practical preparation

Read through the play several times before you begin.

Photocopy sufficient copies of the play and, using a holepunch and bootlace tags, put the pages together to form a book.

Photocopy the rehearsal diary on pages 18–22, enough for one set per child.

Practical casting

This play is suitable for a wide age range.

The Narrators need to be confident readers, who can maintain a spoken rhythm. The narration can be shared in the following ways:
* Between several readers who take one line each.
* By a few readers speaking in unison.
* By a few readers dividing the blocks of speech between them.

Big One, Middle One, Little One: Three children, traditionally one brother and two sisters, but can depend very much on your group. Obviously, they must be distinguishable in size and age, and need to be able performers.

Grandfather: A sizeable part, which could be performed by an older child or an adult leader.

Deer, braves, hunters, chiefs, small animals: All these other characters are non-speaking, but could accommodate a large cast from the very youngest to the oldest.

Practical props

1 woodcarving
1 beaded necklace
2 decorated bags as if made out of skins
1 long length of blue cloth
1 large piece of bark
1 baby doll

Practical staging

You will need a large enough space to have four distinct areas:
* Narrator's space
* Grandfather's wigwam
* The forest where the children are walking
* An area where the large piece of bark is put in preparation for the baby.

A suitable backdrop would be a night sky, studded with stars and the moon. Against that, long triangular pieces of brown paper can be unfolded to act as Grandfather's wigwam—

or you might well find that one of the children has a lightweight wigwam that you can use. Cover the floor with leaves and twigs to add to the atmosphere.

Practical start

Introduce the idea of setting the Christmas story in a different culture. First of all, brainstorm with the group the main elements of the Christmas story and write them up on a large sheet of paper—for example, shepherds, stable, star, wise men. Against each suggestion, ask them to think of an alternative way to explain who these people or things are, to someone who might not have any understanding or concept of, for example, a shepherd. The Wycliffe Bible Translators might be useful people to contact, as this is a problem they regularly come across. They can be contacted at:

Wycliffe Bible Translators
Horsleys Green
High Wycombe
Buckinghamshire
HP14 3XL

Then explain that your choice of a Christmas play will do just that—it will explain the nub of the Christmas story in a new way. Some things you might need to know about North American Indians are:

* They once lived on the Great Plains of Western America, across what we now call the United States and Canada.
* They lived in tents called tepees or wigwams, which were made out of long poles, tied at the top and dug into the earth. The poles were covered in buffalo hides.
* Lots of animals, such as deer, wild turkeys, hares and rabbits, lived on the plains.
* A baby was called a papoose. He travelled in a special bag, which had a board at the back. During the night the papoose was hung up in his bag and tied to a tepee pole, to keep him off the damp ground.

Introduce the plot of the play before reading the text with the children.

Practical plot

One night, three Native American children are walking through the forest to visit their grandfather. They have made some special presents to give to him.

As they walk, they remember some of the stories that their grandfather has told them in the past, of how a special baby was born in the forest, and braves and hunters and great chiefs came to worship him. The youngest child

wonders whether they will see anything amazing in the forest and, as he walks, he suddenly spots some deer, who appear to be praying. His elder brother and sister laugh at the idea, but later on, the middle child spots some other deer who look as though they might be praying. At last they reach their grandfather's wigwam and he tells them the story they have been recollecting. However, the ending of the story is different, as Grandfather suggests that what the younger children have seen may well indeed be true.

Grandfather's Wigwam

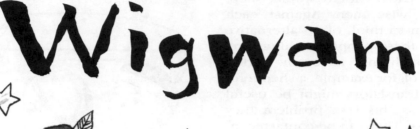

Cast

Narrators
Big One
Little One
Braves and hunters
Great chiefs

Grandfather
Middle One
Deer
Mother

Narrators: One dark evening, long forgotten,
On the North American plain lands,
Lived a tribe of Indian families,
Lived a tribe, each in a wigwam.
One dark evening, stars were twinkling.

Deep within the wooded forest,
Deep beneath the forest branches,
Walked a little group of children,
Walked a brother and two sisters,
Taking presents to their grandfather.

Little One: How far is it to Grandfather's house?

Middle One: Not very far.

Big One: I do hope Grandfather likes his woodcarving.

Middle One: I'm sure he will. He'll know that you have made it for him, whittling the wood and shaping it. Of course he will like it.

Big One: And he will like the beaded necklace you have made for him.

60

Little One: It took us ages to fashion and paint the beads.

Middle One: And to collect the feathers to hang from the cord.

Big One: Grandfather will like all these things.

Middle One: Look, there are some hickory nuts. Let's collect them and give them to him as well.

Narrators: So the children bent to gather,
From the forest's piney floor,
Nuts of every shape and colour,
Gifts of love to give their grandfather,
On that special Christmas evening,
In the North American plain lands,
As the dusk began to fall,
As the stars began to sparkle,
High above the forest floor.

Big One: Look how round the moon is tonight.

Middle One: Look how brightly the stars shine.

Little One: It's because it's a special night.

Big One: Do you think Grandfather will tell us some more stories?

Middle One: Like last year? How once, a long time ago, a tiny baby wrapped in rabbit skins was found rocking in the bark of a tree.

Big One: And how hunter braves, with their bows and arrows, their knives and tomahawks, found him in the forest.

Middle One: And just as they wondered who the baby was, they heard singing, coming from above the pine trees, and saw strange creatures dancing in the stars.

Little One: How wonderful! Maybe we will see something amazing tonight.

Big One: I don't think so, Little One. All of that happened a long time ago, if it happened at all.

Middle One: It's probably just one of Grandfather's stories. Come on.

(The children exit)

CAROL: The rocking carol

(During the singing of the carol, enter a woman and her baby. Indian braves enter and gather round the baby. Or, two of the braves could rock the 'baby' between a strip of fur, while the others watch and sing. Then women and braves exit)

(Enter children and narrators)

Narrators: So the children walked on further,
In between the forest's pine trees,
Telling tales they'd heard from Grandfather,
Telling tales, some half forgotten,
Telling tales of special moments
Tales of much delight and wonder.

Little One: How quiet it is in the forest.

Middle One: It is because it is dark.

Big One: Do keep up, Little One. Grandfather will be waiting for us.

(The two eldest move on, but Little One lingers and, as s/he does so, some deer enter and kneel down, touching their heads on the ground)

Little One: Look!

Middle One: Come on, Little One!

Big One: We've no time.

Little One: But you must come and see!

(As the two eldest return, the deer exit)

Big One: What? What is it you have called us back for?

Little One: There were some deer!

Middle One: So? There are always deer in the forest.

Little One:	But these were kneeling down and praying.
Big One:	Don't be so silly, Little One!
Middle One:	Of course they weren't praying! Deer don't pray!
Little One:	But they were kneeling. And it is a special night.
Big One:	What nonsense, Little One. Deer often kneel!
Middle One:	But to eat the grass—not to pray.

(Exit children. Enter narrators)

Narrators:	So the children walked on further,
	Through the middle of the forest,
	Keeping safe upon the pathway
	Shining brightly in the moonlight,
	On that special Christmas evening.

(Enter assembly of braves to help sing the carol)

CAROL: Silent Night

Little One:	I don't think I have ever seen the moon as big and round as it is tonight.
Big One:	It is a winter moon, Little One. The winter moon is always big and round.
Middle One:	You are right, though, Little One. The moon does seem to be especially bright tonight. I can remember Grandfather saying that the baby the hunters found wrapped in rabbit skins shone more brightly than the winter moon. And that great chiefs left their tribes to travel across the plains to find him.
Little One:	What did they do then?
Big One:	Grandfather says they knelt down in front of him, and gave him presents.
Little One:	What sort of presents? A woodcarving and a beaded necklace like we've made for Grandfather?
Middle One:	Maybe. Who knows? Some fur, perhaps?
Big One:	If I were a chief, I would bring a rawhide shield.

Middle One:	And I would bring a rattle made of deer hooves, or a bird-bone flute.
Little One:	And I would make him a rawhide ball, stuffed with moss, or a bear-claw necklace. Or perhaps a medicine bundle for when he's older, to keep him safe.
Big One:	And if I were a great chief, I would bring my finest horse, and we could ride together across the top of the world.
Middle One:	But hurry! Enough of this chatter. We are nearly at the lake! We are nearly at Grandfather's.

(The two eldest rush off. As they do so, enter the deer, with a strip of lightweight material, held at either end to represent the lake. The deer kneel down in front of the lake and begin to drink)

| **Little One:** | But wait! Wait for me! Come and have a look! The deer have returned, and they *are* praying. |

(The deer exit, but not before Middle One has caught a glimpse of them, before being followed by Big One)

Little One:	Did you see? You did see, didn't you? The deer were praying.
Middle One:	Yes, I saw. And I suppose it could be true, but I doubt it. Deer really do not do that sort of thing, you know, Little One.
Big One:	You are both being silly. Deer do not pray. They were drinking water from the lake. They always drink that way. I have often seen them. Stop wasting time with such nonsense. Let's go to Grandfather's.

(Exit children. During this carol or the succeeding narration, the wigwam-type base could be erected. Enter Grandfather)

CAROL: Girls and Boys, Leave Your Toys

Narrators:	So the children walked by the lakeside On the last part of their journey, Sometimes running, sometimes skipping, Rushing on to see their Grandfather, Clutching tightly precious presents, Guided by the watchful moonlight, Guided by the stars in heaven, On that very special evening.

(Grandfather is sitting crosslegged outside his tent. When the children enter, he stands up to greet them)

Children:	Hello, Grandfather.
Grandfather:	Hello, my dear children. My big one, my middle one and my little one.
Big One:	Here, Grandfather. I've brought a present for you.
Grandfather:	What is it? Whatever can it be? *(Feeling it within the cloth)* I know! It's a hide scraper!
Children:	No!
Grandfather:	A lacrosse bat?
Children:	No! It isn't a lacrosse bat!
Grandfather:	I don't know! I give up. *(Opening present)* Oh, it's a woodcarving! It's so beautifully made, too! Where did you get it from?
Big One:	I made it!
Grandfather:	You did! It's magnificent! The best woodcarving in the world!
Middle One:	And this is from us, Grandfather.

Little One:	We made it together. It's a…
Big/Middle One:	Shhh!
Grandfather:	*(Opening present)* A beaded necklace! What a surprise! Thank you, my dear children. And now I must find a place of honour for my woodcarving, and try on my beaded necklace. What would you like to do, my dears?
Children:	A story, Grandfather! Please tell us a story!
Grandfather:	A story. Ah yes! A special story on this special night.
Little One:	I told you it was a special night.
Big/Middle One:	Shh! Tell us a story, Grandfather.
Grandfather:	And so I will. I will tell you a story that my grandfather told me, and his grandfather told him. One day I hope that you will tell your children this story too. On such a night as this, long, long ago, a very special baby was born into the world. His father was the Great, Great Chief, who lives in heaven. He was born into a world that was like the deepest, darkest forest—a place where wild animals roamed, ready to attack at any moment. He did not have a wigwam of his own, or a cradleboard to keep him safe. Instead, his mother put him to sleep in the rounded bark of a tree and covered him up with rabbit skin.

(During this speech, enter mother and baby again. She puts the baby in the rounded bark of the tree)

Suddenly the moon shone, large and round, casting its light on the face of the tiny baby. The wind blew gently through the forest and, as it blew, the branches of the trees knocked together, like the beat of the tom-tom.

(Sound of drumbeat)

The sound of the branches drifted through the forest. The hunters and braves heard the sound and followed it, until they found the baby.

(Enter hunters and braves as if following the sound. Then they kneel before the baby)

As soon as they saw him, they knew he was the son of the Great, Great Chief and they laid down their knives and their shields and knelt down before him. But the beat kept on, through the forest and across the plains. The great chiefs of all the tribes left their buffalo and their wigwams and followed the sound. They brought presents to give him, furs and feathers, beads and skins.

(Enter the great chiefs with presents. They kneel before the baby)

They came to worship the son of the Great, Great Chief who had brought light to the deep, dark forest. And some people say that on this special night, all the kind and peaceful animals in the forest kneel down and remember the son of the Great, Great Chief who was born long ago.

(Enter 'animals' who kneel before the baby)

CAROL: Away in a Manger

Narrators: So this ends our Christmas story
In the darkness of the forest,
Where a little tiny baby
Came to live among the darkness,
Came to bring some light and wonder
To the people of the plain lands,
To the hunters and the braves,
To the great chiefs far away.
Where this little tiny baby,
Only son of God in heaven,
Came to bring us peace and justice,
Came to show us how to live,
Came to be our friend and brother,
Came to show us God in heaven.
Jesus came to live among us
On that special Christmas night.

CAROL: Come and Join the Celebration